Thank you to the children who suggested their favourite
amazing facts: Tom Bourne-Cox, Lyra Chilton, Rudy
Chilton, Calla Mackenzie, Evan Mackenzie — C.B.

For my daughter Rosie who is forever
on the hunt for new facts – S.J.

Written by Catherine Brereton.
Illustrations by Steve James.
Front cover design by Thy Bui.

Red Shed would also like to thank author Clive Gifford and
illustrator Chris Dickason for use of some content from *Fake News*.

First published in Great Britain in 2021 by Red Shed, part of Farshore

An imprint of HarperCollins*Publishers*
1 London Bridge Street
London SE1 9GF
www.farshore.co.uk

HarperCollins*Publishers*
1st Floor, Watermarque Building, Ringsend Road, Dublin 4, Ireland

Copyright © HarperCollins*Publishers* Limited 2021

ISBN 978 0 00 849217 5
Printed and Bound in the UK using 100% Renewable Electricity
at CPI Group (UK) Ltd.
003
A CIP catalogue is available from the British Library.

MIX
Paper from
responsible sources
FSC™ C007454

AMAZING FACTS EVERY 6 YEAR OLD NEEDS TO KNOW

RED SHED

Whether you love animals or adventure, science or sport, you'll find LOADS of weird and wonderful facts ...

What animal was once a police traffic officer?

How many Earths could fit inside the Sun?

How many teeth does a great white shark have?

Whose wee is recycled to make drinking water?

Read on to find out the answers and lots more awesome information ...

A crocodile cannot
stick its tongue out.

If a donkey and a zebra have
a baby, it's called a zonkey.

There is a World's Ugliest Dog competition every year in the United States.

Children grow faster in springtime.

Humans are the only animals that have chins.

Some people's sweat is coloured bright yellow, blue or green.

Some perfumes have
whale poo in them.

You can buy a perfume that
smells like bacon.

Buzzzzz . . . a honeybee's wings move up and down 230 times a second.

It takes 12 bees their whole life to produce a single teaspoon of honey.

**Butterflies taste food
with their feet.**

The first skyscrapers in the 1880s were just 10–20 storeys high. Today, the tallest skyscraper has over 160 storeys!

On Kaua'i, Hawaii, no one
is allowed to build anything
taller than a palm tree.

A day on the planet Venus is longer than its year.

More than a million Earths could fit inside the Sun.

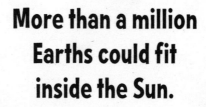

Uranus is the coldest planet in the Solar System.

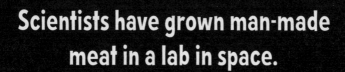

Scientists have grown man-made meat in a lab in space.

There is a world record for the llama high jump. A llama called Caspa holds the record, at 1.13 metres.

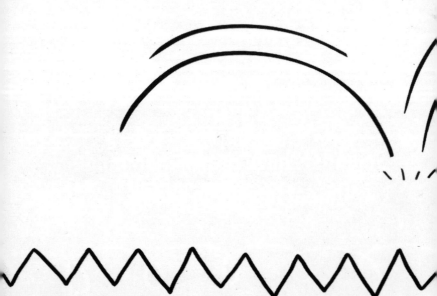

Hippos make a special sticky sweat that works like sunscreen.

Herrings talk to each other by farting.

Elephants use their trunks to say hello. It's like a cuddle.

Baby elephants sometimes
suck their trunks . . . a bit like
us sucking our thumbs.

They also use their trunks to smell,
breathe, drink, shout and grab things.

Cows that have been given names produce more milk than others.

Anastasia

In ancient China, some royalty
kept dogs up their sleeves,
ready to jump out and scare
anyone who might attack them.

Baby alligators bark when they are ready to hatch out of their eggs.

The horned lizard squirts blood out of its eyes.

The smallest reptile on Earth is a chameleon the size of a seed.

**Some cars can run
on reused cooking oil.**

A car is made up of around 30,000 separate parts.

It takes a spider
about an hour
to spin a web.

Some spiders build a new
web every day. If the web
gets broken, they eat it.

The Goliath birdeater is the world's biggest spider. It's as big as a dinner plate.

It mainly eats mice, frogs and lizards, but sometimes eats birds.

A newborn baby red kangaroo is small enough to fit in a teaspoon.

Most kangaroos are left-handed.

Goldfish sleep with their eyes open as they have no eyelids.

Zzzzzzzz

Goldfish teeth are in the back of their throats.

An orange will float in water, but if you peel it, it sinks.

Kangaroos cannot jump backwards.

**The closest relatives of the dinosaur
Tyrannosaurus rex alive today are . . .
the chicken and the ostrich!**

A prehistoric snake called Titanoboa
was over 13 metres long and
weighed as much as a car.

Fossilized dinosaur poo
is called coprolite.

Jingle Bells was the first song to be played in space.

Penguins shoot a stream of poo far away from the nest. They make so much poo that it can be seen from space!

A dog called Bosco was once the mayor (a kind of town leader) of a town in California, United States.

A monkey called Santisuk was a traffic police officer in Thailand.

Russell the dog had a job listening to children read in a school in Scotland.

Octopuses squirt ink when they are scared or angry.

The mantis shrimp punches its prey with its big strong claws.

Fruit flies, a monkey, dogs, mice, rats, a rabbit and a cat all travelled into space before humans did.

A blue whale's tongue can weigh as much as an elephant.

The poo an elephant produces in one day weighs about the same as six six-year-old children.

Underwater hockey is sometimes called octopush.

A German athlete, Christopher Irmscher, ran a hurdles race while wearing flippers.

The shapes on a football are 12 pentagons and 20 hexagons.

There is a floating football pitch in the sea in Singapore.

Sharks keep wearing out their teeth and growing new ones all their life.

Human teeth are just as strong as shark teeth.

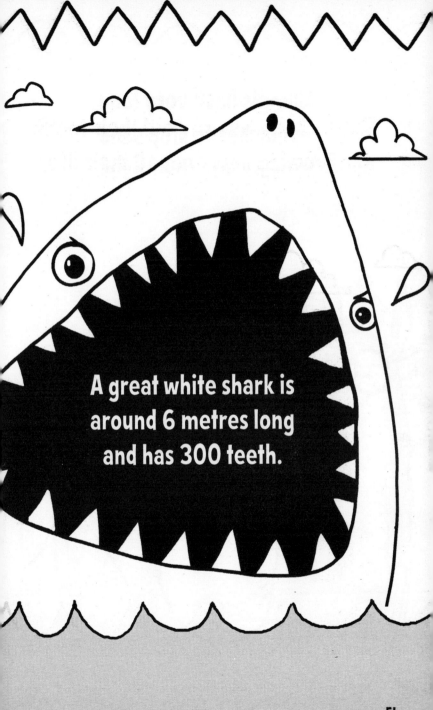

A great white shark is around 6 metres long and has 300 teeth.

Camels have very long eyelashes to stop sand blowing into their eyes.

Sheep and goats have rectangular pupils. Ours are round.

An astronaut's toilet fixes onto their bottom – the toilet works like a vacuum cleaner and sucks the poo and wee away.

Their wee is recycled to make clean drinking water.

Astronauts' food floats all over the place inside their spacecraft if they're not careful to hold on to it.

In 2001 a pizza restaurant on Earth delivered pizza to astronauts in space!

Russia's Trans-Siberian Railway is the world's longest railway and crosses a whopping 3,901 bridges.

3,901

Russia's biggest museum has around 50 cats living there as guards.

The world's biggest cat, the Siberian tiger, lives in Russia.

Turtles were living at the same time as the dinosaurs.

A teaspoon of seawater might contain a million sea creatures.

Some male fish whistle to impress a female.

Some animals that live in the dark at the bottom of the sea make their own light.

There is an orchestra in Austria whose instruments are vegetables!

They include carrot recorders, radish flutes and pumpkin drums.

In 2010, the city of Sydney, Australia, held a concert for an audience of dogs.

Stegosaurus was as big as a bus but its brain was only as big as a hotdog.

Many dinosaurs were smaller than people.

Growing pineapples was once a way for extremely rich people in Britain and parts of Europe to show off.

A museum of tea in China is shaped like an enormous teapot.

Ice cream was once called cream ice.

Some caterpillars look a lot like poo, to put off predators that might eat them.

**The orchid mantis looks like
a beautiful flower to trick its prey.**

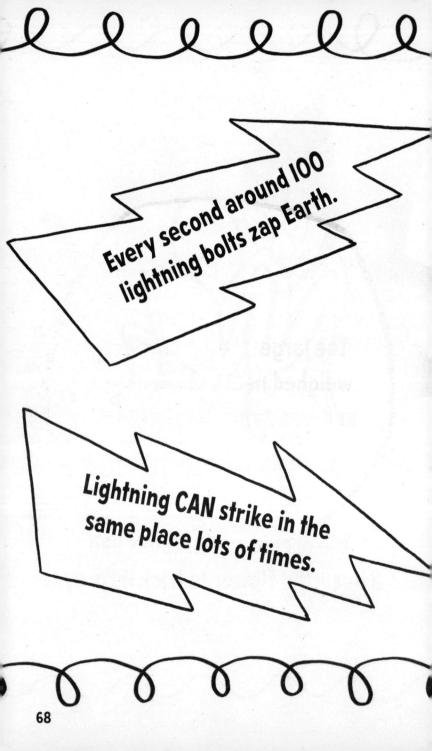

Every second around 100 lightning bolts zap Earth.

Lightning CAN strike in the same place lots of times.

The largest hailstone ever weighed nearly a kilogram and was as big as a football.

The world's tallest cake was made in Indonesia and was an amazing 33 metres tall. That's as high as 28 six year olds!

A piece of cake more than 4,000 years old was found in Egypt.

A cheetah is the fastest runner, and can go more than 100 kilometres an hour.

The fastest person has run 44.72 kilometres an hour.

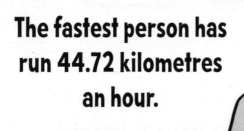

A sailfish swims even faster – 110 kilometres an hour.

A peregrine falcon can dive at a speedy 322 kilometres an hour.

Sea lions are the only mammals (except humans) that we know can move in time to music.

Moles can do forward rolls.

**Toads usually walk or run,
whereas frogs leap and jump.**

Your nose and ears carry on growing for your whole life.

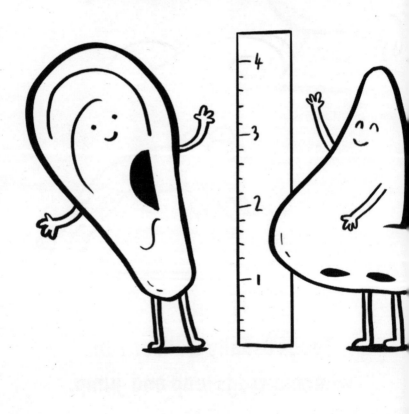

When you blush, the inside of your stomach turns red too.

You can't tickle yourself.

Around half a million mice live on the London Underground.

Foxes and pigeons have been spotted travelling by tube.

A lion's roar can be heard up to 5 kilometres away.

Every zebra has a different pattern of stripes.

You have the same number of bones in your neck as a giraffe.

There are more chickens in the world than any other kind of bird.

A hen can lay about
300 eggs in a year.

Pig Beach in the Bahamas
is home to a herd of
swimming pigs.

The world's tallest sandcastle was 17.65 metres tall and was built in Germany in 2019.

Sugar and salt are actually types of sand.

Sand can be white, golden, brown, grey, black, red or even pink.

**In Malaysia, there is
a five-star hotel for cats.**

Cats can't taste anything that's sweet.

Cats can sweat through their paws.

People have been keeping cats as pets for 9,500 years.

In 2019, a solid gold toilet was on display in a palace in England. It was stolen and has never been found.

There is enough gold buried in
Earth's rocks to cover the whole
planet with a layer of it.

Japanese snow monkeys have learned to bathe in hot springs to keep warm and relax.

Some monkeys in Thailand teach their young to floss their teeth.

A spider monkey can use its extra-long tail to pick up something as small as a peanut.

Tinned peaches and bacon squares were part of the first meal eaten on the Moon.

Astronaut Alan Shepard played golf on the Moon – and the golf balls are still up there.

There are **80 LEGO®** bricks for every person in the world.

LEGO® produces more wheels every year than any car maker.